Fun Fan Facts:
The Unofficial NBA Edition

Minnesota Timberwolves

Everything Young Timberwolves Fans Should Know

By: Jake Liam

Dedication

For every Wolves fan who stayed loud through the long winters. Your time is coming. Let's hunt.

THE NBA BY THE NUMBERS

MOST NBA CHAMPIONSHIPS[*]

- CELTICS (18) [†]
- LAKERS (17)
- WARRIORS (7)
- BULLS (6)
- SPURS (5)

As of the 2024-25 Season. †One Trophy = 4 Championships.

NBA HISTORY SNAPSHOT

1946 — NBA Founded
1954 — Shot Clock Introduced
1979 — 3-Point Line Added
2023 — NBA Cup Introduced

BIG NUMBERS

$156 million
Stephen Curry's est. earnings in the 24-25 season

7'7"
Tallest player in NBA history (Gheorghe Mureșan & Manute Bol)

30 | 4 | 82

30 — Teams Competing in the NBA

4 — Playoff Rounds

82 — Games Per Season

MINNESOTA TIMBERWOLVES
IN THE NBA

- FOUNDED: 1989[†]
- NBA TITLES: 0
- CONFERENCE TITLES: 0[*]

16 Playoff Appearances

*† Founding dates are complicated & may cause arguments at Thanksgiving. Ask someone born before color TV. All Titles reflect pre-relocation franchise history. * As of 2024-25 Season.*

NBA ALL-TIME MVP LEADERS

KAREEM ABDUL-JABBAR (6) ★ MICHAEL JORDAN (5) ★ BILL RUSSELL (5)

EASTERN CONFERENCE

Atlantic – **Celtics**
Atlantic – **Nets**
Atlantic – **Knicks**
Atlantic – **76ers**
Atlantic – **Raptors**
Central – **Bulls**
Central – **Cavaliers**
Central – **Pistons**
Central – **Pacers**
Central – **Bucks**
Southeast – **Hawks**
Southeast – **Hornets**
Southeast – **Heat**
Southeast – **Magic**
Southeast – **Wizards**

WESTERN CONFERENCE

Pacific – **Lakers**
Pacific – **Clippers**
Pacific – **Warriors**
Pacific – **Suns**
Pacific – **Kings**
Northwest – **Nuggets**
Northwest – **Timberwolves**
Northwest – **Thunder**
Northwest – **Trail Blazers**
Northwest – **Jazz**
Southwest – **Mavericks**
Southwest – **Rockets**
Southwest – **Spurs**
Southwest – **Pelicans**
Southwest – **Grizzlies**

Introduction

Welcome, fans! Whether you're new to cheering for the Minnesota Timberwolves or you've been bleeding the team colors your whole life, this book is packed with fun, exciting facts about your favorite team. Get ready to impress your friends and family with everything you know about the Timberwolves.

Quick Timeout

This book is packed with stats. Like, A LOT of stats. Every fact was checked, double-checked, and triple-checked. But here's the thing about basketball history: not everyone agrees on everything. Ask someone who watched games before color TV and someone who grew up with instant replay and you'll get two completely different answers. My dad, stepdad, uncle, and grandpa all argued about the same fact. Four people. Four answers. All of them think they're right. So if you spot something that doesn't match what you've heard, congratulations. You might be a bigger fan than the people who helped make this book. And honestly? That's pretty cool.

HOW IT WORKS

THE SEASON
82 Games. One Goal.
Each team plays 82 games.
Win enough to make the
Playoffs.
Every game counts!

PLAYOFFS
30 Teams. 16 Make It.
8 per conference make the playoffs.
Win=Advance | Lose=Go Home
Best record
gets home court!

PLAYOFF ROUNDS
Best of 7. Win 4 or Go Home.
4 rounds of pure pressure.
Every series is do-or-die!

OVERTIME?
5 More Minutes.
Keep playing until
someone pulls ahead.
No ties. Ever.

THE FINALS
One Series. One Champion.
Winner lifts the Trophy.
Legend status unlocked.

How the NBA Works

At first glance, basketball feels simple. Ten players. One ball. Two hoops. Go.

Then the NBA adds the layers.

An 82-game regular season. A draft where bad teams pick first. Playoffs that last two full months. Superstars who can change everything with one trade. Dynasties that rise, fall, and rise again.

And somehow, it all works.

The NBA is built on one big idea: every team gets a chance to reset, reload, and rise again. No relegation. No dropping down to a lower league. Just basketball, every night, from October through June.

It is a league designed for drama, stars, and comebacks. And once you understand the flow, it is impossible to stop watching.

The League Setup

The NBA has 30 teams, spread across the United States and Canada. Those teams are split into two conferences:

- Eastern Conference
- Western Conference

Each conference has three divisions, mostly based on geography. Divisions matter for scheduling, but not as much as they used to.

Every team plays 82 regular season games, usually from October through April. Home games. Road games. Back-to-back nights. Long road trips. The season is a marathon before the sprint even starts.

Win games, and you climb the standings. Lose too many, and the pressure builds fast.

How Games Are Played

An NBA game has four quarters, each lasting 12 minutes. That means 48 minutes of game time, plus timeouts, free throws, and the occasional coach argument that adds another 20 minutes nobody planned for.

Scoring is simple:

- A shot inside the three-point line is worth 2 points
- A shot beyond the arc is worth 3 points
- Free throws are worth 1 point

If the score is tied at the end of regulation, the game goes to overtime, which lasts 5 minutes. Still tied? Another overtime. Keep going until someone wins.

There is a shot clock too. Teams have 24 seconds to take a shot. No standing around. No holding the ball forever. Keep it moving.

The Regular Season Race

The regular season is long for a reason. It tests everything.

Depth. Health. Focus. Patience.

Teams play opponents from both conferences, but they face conference rivals more often. By the end of the season, each conference's top teams have earned their playoff spots the hard way.

The goal is simple: make the playoffs. But there is a twist.

The NBA Cup

In 2023, the NBA added something new to the middle of the season. Something with actual stakes. They called it the In-Season Tournament, now known as the NBA Cup.

It works like this: Every team plays a small group stage during November and December, with special court designs that look like nothing else in basketball. The best teams advance to a knockout round held in Las Vegas.

The winners split a prize pool. Players earn bonus money. And for the first time, a team could lift a trophy before the playoffs even started.

Some fans are still warming up to it. Some players love it. But the moment a team starts treating it seriously and a crowd shows up buzzing in December, it feels like something.

Which, honestly, sounds about right.

The Play-In Tournament

Instead of sending the top eight teams from each conference straight to the playoffs, the NBA added something new. The Play-In Tournament.

Here is how it works:

- Teams ranked 1 through 6 in each conference are safe
- Teams ranked 7 through 10 fight for the final two playoff spots

The 7 and 8 seeds have an advantage. Win once and you are in. Lose and you still get one more shot. The 9 and 10 seeds have to win twice in a row just to earn a first-round matchup.

It turns the end of the season into a sprint. Every game suddenly matters more. Fans love it. Coaches age rapidly.

The NBA Playoffs

Once the playoffs begin, everything tightens.

Sixteen teams enter. Eight from each conference. Every round is a best-of-seven games series. That means the first team to win four games moves on:

- First Round
- Conference Semifinals
- Conference Finals
- NBA Finals

Home-court advantage matters. Crowds get louder. Rotations get shorter. Superstars play heavier minutes. One bad quarter can flip a series. One great performance can define a career.

By the time the NBA Finals arrive in June, only two teams are left. One from the East. One from the West.

Four wins away from a championship. Four wins away from history.

The NBA Draft: Hope Begins Here

Here is where the NBA gets clever. Every summer, new players enter the league through the NBA Draft. Teams take turns selecting college players, international stars, and teenagers straight out of high school.

The teams that finished with the worst records get the best odds to pick early through the Draft Lottery. It is not guaranteed, but it gives struggling franchises a real shot at changing their future with one pick.

That means one bad season does not doom you forever. It might actually change everything. Some franchises are rebuilt by a single draft night moment.

Hope shows up wearing a new jersey.

No Relegation. All Pressure.

Unlike many global sports leagues, NBA teams never drop down to a lower league. They always stay in the NBA.

That does not mean there is no pressure.

Fans remember losing seasons. Owners make changes. Coaches get replaced. Players get traded. Every year is a test of direction, patience, and belief.

Stars, Systems, and Showtime

The NBA is famous for its stars. But stars do not win alone.

Teams need chemistry. Coaches need systems. Role players need to deliver on the biggest stages. One injury. One hot streak. One trade deadline deal. Any of it can flip a season.

That balance between individual brilliance and team basketball is what makes the league special.

Fast breaks. Buzzer-beaters. Game 7s. And moments that get replayed forever. That is the NBA.

Once you get the flow, it is pure electricity.

Minnesota Timberwolves Facts

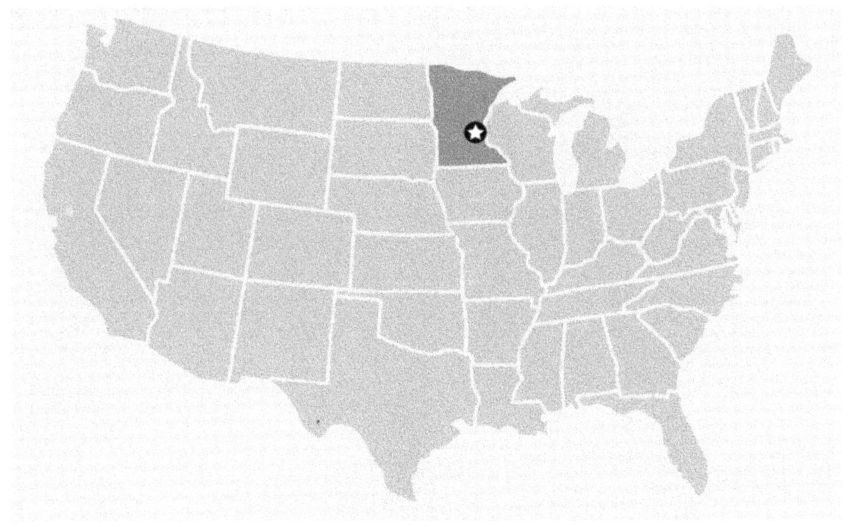

Home City

Minneapolis, Minnesota

Home City Metro Area Population

about 3.7 million

Home Arena

Target Center

Max Capacity: 18,978

Famous Local Food

Jucy Lucy burgers, wild rice soup, walleye, hotdish

Conference / Division

Western / Northwest

Chapter 1: Born in the Land of 10,000 Lakes

1. The Day the NBA Came North

Minnesota had not seen professional basketball in nearly three decades. The Minneapolis Lakers, the original dynasty of the NBA, had packed their bags and headed to Los Angeles all the way back in 1960, leaving the state with nothing but cold winters and a lot of unresolved feelings about it. Then, on April 22, 1987, two local businessmen named Harvey Ratner and Marv Wolfenson handed the NBA a check for $32.5 million, and just like that, professional basketball had a Minnesota return date.

The team would not tip off until November 3, 1989, which meant fans had nearly two full years to get excited. They used every minute of it. Minnesota was a state that had always loved its sports. The Vikings, the Twins, the North Stars. But basketball? Basketball had been gone so long it felt like a relative nobody had seen in thirty years suddenly showing up at Thanksgiving. A little awkward. A lot welcome.

The first ever game was a road loss to the Seattle SuperSonics. The home opener five days later was a loss to the Chicago Bulls, who brought along a young man named Michael Jordan just to make sure nobody felt too comfortable. But none of that mattered. Basketball was back in the Land of 10,000 Lakes, and Minnesota was ready to howl.

2. Why Timberwolves? The Name That Beat the Polars

Before a single game had been played, before a single jersey had been designed, someone had to figure out what to call this thing. So the organizers did something surprisingly fun. They held a public naming contest and asked the whole state to get involved. Over 6,000 entries poured in, suggesting 1,284 different nicknames for a team that did not even exist yet. Minnesotans take their identity seriously.

Two names rose to the top: Timberwolves and Polars. Both made sense. Minnesota is famous for its brutal winters, its vast forests, and its wild northern landscape. A polar bear would have been intimidating. A timberwolf would be, too. To break the tie, the organizers did something almost comically democratic. They asked all 842 city councils across the state to vote. The result was not even close. Timberwolves won by nearly two to one.

It turned out to be the perfect choice. Minnesota is home to the largest gray wolf population in the continental United States outside of Alaska. The International Wolf Center, one of the only facilities in the world dedicated entirely to wolf research and education, sits in Ely, Minnesota. This was not just a cool name. It was a genuine piece of who Minnesota is, and fans connected with it immediately. The Polars were forgotten before the ink was dry.

3. The Metrodome: The Loudest Temporary Home in NBA History

Before Target Center existed, the Timberwolves needed somewhere to play. The answer was the Hubert H. Humphrey Metrodome, a giant domed stadium built for football and baseball that had absolutely no business hosting NBA games. The ceilings were enormous, the sightlines were built for a completely different sport, and the whole setup had a slightly chaotic energy that you either loved or found deeply confusing.

Imagine this: It is April 17, 1990. You are one of 49,551 people crammed into a domed football stadium to watch a basketball game. The noise bounces off the dome ceiling and comes back at you from seventeen directions at once. You can barely see the court from some of those seats. The Timberwolves are losing to the Denver Nuggets. And yet, every single one of those 49,551 people is there, loud, proud, and completely invested in a team that has won just 22 games all season.

That crowd of 49,551 set a record at the time for the largest attendance at an NBA game. Not bad for a first year team playing in a football stadium. What it showed was something important about Minnesota fans: they did not need a winning team to show up. They just needed a team. The Timberwolves would give them plenty of heartbreak over the years ahead, but the fans had already proven they were in for the long haul from day one.

4. A Real Home: Target Center Opens Downtown

For the 1990-91 season, the Timberwolves moved into a proper home. Target Center opened in downtown Minneapolis as a purpose-built NBA arena, and it changed everything about the game day experience. Suddenly there were real sightlines. Real acoustics. A place where basketball felt like basketball was supposed to feel.

The arena seated around 18,800 fans and sat right in the heart of downtown Minneapolis, which meant it became part of the city's identity almost immediately. On game nights, the whole neighborhood lit up. Restaurants filled. Bars packed out. The Timberwolves were not just a basketball team playing in a big room anymore. They were part of the city's fabric, a reason to be downtown, a gathering place for a state that had been waiting a long time for this.

Target Center would go on to host some of the most electric nights in Minnesota sports history, and a few of the most heartbreaking ones too. It would witness Kevin Garnett's first steps as a professional, the chaos of the 2003-04 championship push, and eventually the roar of a new generation of fans watching Anthony Edwards do things that made grown adults call their parents. But in 1990, it was simply a beautiful new arena, and the Timberwolves finally had a home worth showing off.

5. The Draft Pick That Changed Everything

By 1995, the Timberwolves had not made the playoffs once. Not even close. Six seasons in, the best record they had managed was 29 wins. The team was not bad in an interesting way. It was bad in a very ordinary, forgettable way. Then came June 28, 1995, and everything changed.

With the fifth overall pick in the NBA Draft, Minnesota selected a 19-year-old kid from Chicago who had skipped college entirely and was heading straight from high school to the NBA. That had not happened in 20 years. His name was Kevin Garnett, and if you are a Timberwolves fan of a certain age, that name still does something to your heart. KG was not just a talented prospect. He was a 6-foot-11 force of nature who could do things that big men simply were not supposed to be able to do. He passed. He handled the ball. He defended everything that moved. He talked more trash than anyone in the league and backed every word of it up.

The city of Minneapolis did not fully understand what had just landed in its lap. More on that in Chapter 2. But what the 1995 draft did was give a struggling franchise its identity, its cornerstone, and its future all at once. It took a couple of years for everything to come together, but the day they called Kevin Garnett's name was the day the Timberwolves stopped being an expansion punchline and started becoming something real.

6. Kevin Garnett: The Big Ticket (1995-2007, 2015-2016)

There is a version of Timberwolves history where Kevin Garnett never happens. Where the 1995 draft goes differently, where some other franchise gets the fifth pick, and where Minnesota spends another decade finishing last and apologizing about it. Instead, Garnett happened. And nothing was ever the same.

He arrived as a 19-year-old from Chicago who had skipped college entirely. The NBA had not seen anyone go straight from high school to the draft in 20 years, and plenty of people thought it was a mistake. Garnett spent the next decade making those people look extremely foolish. He stood 6 feet 11 inches tall, could guard every position on the floor, passed like a point guard, and played every single minute of every single game like the building was on fire and he was personally responsible for putting it out. His intensity was not just a personality trait. It was a weapon. Opposing players would report feeling unsettled by the time they left the court. That is not an accident.

By the time his first chapter in Minnesota ended in 2007, Garnett had made 15 All-Star teams, won the league MVP award in 2004, and led the Wolves to eight straight playoff appearances. He was inducted into the Naismith Basketball Hall of Fame in 2020. He came back to Minnesota for a final season in 2015-16 to end his career where it started, because of course he did. His statue, when it inevitably goes up outside Target Center, will probably look like it is screaming at someone. That is entirely appropriate.

Kevin Garnett slams home a dunk for the Minnesota Timberwolves. Power at the rim. Fire in his voice. "KG" played every second like the game depended on it. Photo: Kevin Garnett dunking for the Minnesota Timberwolves, 2007.

7. Stephon Marbury: The Coney Island Kid (1996-1999)

For two and a half glorious seasons, Stephon Marbury and Kevin Garnett formed one of the most exciting young backcourt and frontcourt pairings in the entire NBA. Marbury was a 20-year-old blur of a point guard out of Brooklyn, New York, drafted by Milwaukee and traded to Minnesota on draft night in exchange for Ray Allen, which in hindsight was a trade that broke the hearts of exactly nobody in Minnesota at the time and broke several hearts much later when people did the math.

Marbury and Garnett were electric together. The Wolves made the playoffs in back-to-back seasons, something the franchise had never done before. The city was excited. The future looked absurdly bright. Then, in the winter of 1999, Marbury asked to be traded. His reasons were numerous and, looking back, actually understandable. He was a kid from a New York neighborhood with zero winter experience, and Minnesota had a way of making a New York winter feel like a warm vacation. He reportedly told people that he had nearly died more than once just trying to get to his own car. He wanted a bigger market, closer family, more endorsements. He wanted out.

The trade happened in March 1999, and it sent shockwaves through the franchise. Wolves fans mourned what could have been. The duo never got to finish what they started, and neither player ever quite reached the heights that seemed inevitable when they were running together in Minneapolis. Marbury eventually became a legend overseas in China, where they built a statue of him and treated him like royalty. Which is a wonderful ending to the story, even if it did not involve a Timberwolves championship. Ray Allen, by the way, won two NBA titles. Just mentioning it.

8. Kevin Love: The Rebounding Machine (2008-2014)

Kevin Love arrived in Minnesota in 2008 looking like a man who had accidentally taken a wrong turn on his way to somewhere more glamorous. He was 20 years old, the son of a former NBA player, and had just been traded on draft night from Memphis to Minnesota in exchange for the third overall pick. He had played exactly one year of college basketball. He had a beard that made him look like he was 35. And he was about to do something to a basketball court in Minnesota that nobody had seen in almost 30 years.

On November 12, 2010, Love scored 31 points and grabbed 31 rebounds in a single game against the New York Knicks. A 30-30 game. The last person to do that in the NBA was Moses Malone in 1982. Love grabbed 15 rebounds in the third quarter alone, which means in a single 12-minute stretch, he corralled nearly as many missed shots as some players grab in an entire game. He finished his time in Minnesota averaging 19.2 points and 12.2 rebounds per game across six seasons. That is not a typo. That is what he did, every single night, for six years, on a team that rarely made the playoffs.

In the 2013-14 season, Love became the first player in NBA history to put up 2,000 points, 900 rebounds, and

100 three-pointers in a single season. He was stretching the floor before stretching the floor was a thing every team demanded. He was a modern big man before the league caught up to what modern big men could be. Minnesota eventually traded him to Cleveland, where he won an NBA championship in 2016. Wolves fans cried. Then they watched him win a ring and decided to be happy for him. Eventually.

9. Karl-Anthony Towns: KAT (2015-2024)

Karl-Anthony Towns arrived in Minnesota as the first overall pick in the 2015 NBA Draft, and the city immediately had a problem. The problem was that Karl-Anthony Towns was too good for a team that was not ready to be good yet. It was like ordering a five-star meal and only having a plastic fork.

KAT was a 7-footer from New Jersey who had grown up partly in the Dominican Republic and had a mother born in the Dominican Republic. He spoke English and Spanish, shot three-pointers like a guard, scored from every spot on the floor, and was named NBA Rookie of the Year in his first season, making him and the previous year's Rookie of the Year, Andrew Wiggins, the first back-to-back rookies from the same team in league history. He was, on paper and in person, a franchise-altering talent. The franchise, unfortunately, took a few years to catch up.

When Anthony Edwards arrived in 2020, everything clicked. KAT and Ant formed a devastating pairing, and the Wolves started winning playoff games for the first time in ages. Towns averaged 22.3 points and 8.1 rebounds per game across his nine seasons in Minnesota. Then, in the autumn of 2024, he was traded to the New York Knicks in exchange for Julius Randle and Donte DiVincenzo. Wolves fans were stunned. KAT was stunned. But the Knicks had been trying to get him for years, and some chapters in a player's story end before anyone is quite ready for them to. His nine seasons gave Minnesota some of its best basketball in a generation. The torch had been officially passed to someone who had very, very strong feelings about who you should bring to Minnesota.

10. Anthony Edwards: Ant-Man (2020-present)

Anthony Edwards was born in Atlanta in 2001, grew up as a running back who could dunk, and was selected first overall by the Minnesota Timberwolves in the 2020 NBA Draft during a draft ceremony that took place over video call because of the pandemic. He joined a team that had not been relevant in years. He was 19. He had no idea he was about to drag an entire franchise back into the spotlight by sheer force of personality.

The numbers are extraordinary. By his third season he was an All-Star. By his fourth he was the engine of a team that went to the Western Conference Finals for the first time since 2004. He averaged 25.9 points per game in 2023-24 and was seventh in MVP voting. In the 2024 playoffs, after Minnesota eliminated the Denver Nuggets in a historic upset, Edwards was interviewed on national television by Charles Barkley, who mentioned he had not been to Minnesota in about 20 years. Edwards told him, without a single second of hesitation, to bring himself to Minnesota. The phrase went viral overnight. It was printed on t-shirts. It became a state motto. A 22-year-old told an NBA legend to come visit his city, and the city loved him even more for it. To see the actual phrase you have to turn this book upside down (bring ya ass).

But the real story is not just the scoring or the dunks or the viral moments. It is the fact that Ant just really loves Minnesota. He stays in the offseason. He invests in the community. He wears the responsibility of being the face of the franchise without flinching. Kevin Garnett was the first Timberwolves player who made the city feel like it had a superstar worth building around. Anthony Edwards is the second. The pack is hunting again.

11. The Season Nobody in Minnesota Will Ever Forget

The 2003-04 Minnesota Timberwolves were not supposed to be this good. They had lost in the first round of the playoffs seven years in a row. Seven. That is not a rough patch. That is a lifestyle. Then general manager Kevin McHale decided enough was enough and completely overhauled the roster around Kevin Garnett, bringing in veteran guard Sam Cassell and swingman Latrell Sprewell to give KG the kind of help he had never had. The result was the best season in franchise history, and it was not particularly close.

Garnett played all 82 games and averaged 24.2 points, 13.9 rebounds, 5.0 assists, 2.2 blocks, and 1.5 steals per game. He won the NBA's Player of the Month award four times in that single season alone. Four times. Most players go their entire careers without winning it once. He was named league MVP in a runaway, becoming the first power forward in 14 years to take the award. The team finished 58-24, the best record in the entire Western Conference, and earned the first division title in franchise history. Wolves fans who had spent the previous decade watching first-round exits had to sit down and process that this was actually happening.

At the All-Star break, with the Wolves sitting at something like 30-10, players were reportedly riding the team bus talking about what the championship parade was going to look like and whether they would get invited to the White House. It was that kind of season. The parade never came, but the joy of that regular season was real, it was earned, and no one can take it away from the fans who lived it.

12. The Night KG Jumped on the Scorer's Table

The 2004 playoffs were the most dramatic postseason run in Timberwolves history, and the moment that defines it happened on May 19, 2004, which was also Kevin Garnett's 28th birthday. Minnesota needed to beat the Sacramento Kings in a winner-take-all Game 7 to reach the Western Conference Finals for the first time ever. KG spent his birthday playing like a man who had been waiting nine years for exactly this moment, because he had. He finished with 32 points, 21 rebounds, and 5 blocks.

Imagine this. The buzzer sounds. The Timberwolves have won. Kevin Garnett, who has played in Minnesota since he was a teenager, who has ground through years of first-round exits and roster instability and never once stopped giving everything, sprints to the scorer's table and leaps on top of it. He pumps his fist. The arena goes completely unhinged. Grown adults in the stands are crying. Players are running around like they won a championship. They had not won a championship. They had won the right to play in the conference finals. That is what 15 years of waiting for a moment does to a fanbase.

Minnesota beat the Denver Nuggets in five games in round one and then survived that epic seven-game war with Sacramento to reach the Western Conference Finals against the Los Angeles Lakers. Shaquille O'Neal and Kobe Bryant's Lakers were loaded, Sam Cassell picked up a hip injury that hampered the series, and the Wolves fell in six games. It was heartbreaking. But Target Center that May was the loudest it had ever been, and Wolves fans who were there will tell their grandchildren about it. Every. Single. Time.

13. The Most Interesting Roster in Franchise History

Here is how you build a championship contender in a single offseason. You take a generational talent who has been underserved for almost a decade. You add a 33-year-old point guard with two championship rings and ice water in his veins. Then, just to keep things interesting, you sign the guy who famously grabbed his head coach by the throat during practice. Welcome to the 2003-04 Minnesota Timberwolves.

Latrell Sprewell had choked his Golden State Warriors coach P.J. Carlesimo in 1997 and had been one of the most polarizing players in the league ever since. People thought bringing him to Minnesota was reckless. What actually happened was that Sprewell and Garnett got along immediately, and Sprewell played some of the best basketball of his career. He averaged just under 20 points a game in the regular season and became a key piece of one of the highest-scoring trios in the league that year alongside Cassell and KG. The team had chemistry that surprised the basketball world.

The season had everything. Cassell doing his now-legendary big-ball dance celebration after big shots. Garnett conducting the defense like a conductor who had also taken up screaming. Flip Saunders making it all work from the sideline. Fred Hoiberg, later a head coach, serving as the perfectly calm veteran presence off the bench. After the season, Sprewell made headlines for rejecting a contract extension by saying he needed to feed his family. The quote became famous. The offer was reportedly worth around $21 million. Latrell Sprewell's family was going to be fine. But the quip became part of NBA folklore forever, which is a fitting ending for the most chaotic beautiful season in Wolves history.

14. Sixty Points and a Mother's Memory

On March 14, 2022, Karl-Anthony Towns went to San Antonio on a road trip and scored 60 points in 36 minutes. He grabbed 17 rebounds. He made 7 of his 11 three-point attempts. He joined Shaquille O'Neal, Karl Malone, Michael Jordan, and Wilt Chamberlain as the only players in NBA history to score 60 points and grab 15 rebounds in a single game. His coach told him at the end of the third quarter, with 56 points already in the bank and the record within reach, to go get 60. Towns went out and got 60. Because of course he did.

The numbers were surreal enough on their own. What made the night unforgettable was what Towns said afterward. He noted quietly that the game had been played exactly two years to the day that his parents had been admitted to a hospital with Covid-19. His father survived. His mother Jacqueline, who he called one of the great joys of his life, did not. Towns had carried that grief publicly and privately for two years, and on the night he put up the greatest individual performance in Timberwolves franchise history, he said simply that his mother was looking down on him.

Towns later broke even that record, dropping 62 points against the Charlotte Hornets in January 2024, becoming the first player in league history to record at least 10 made three-pointers, two-pointers, and free throws in the same game. His teammates doused him in water after the 60-point game. They lost the 62-point game. Nobody said basketball was fair. But both nights belonged to one of the most gifted scorers the franchise has ever seen, and both nights reminded everyone that the numbers on the stat sheet are only part of the story.

15. Taking Down the Champions

The 2024 Western Conference Semifinals were not supposed to happen the way they happened. The Minnesota Timberwolves, led by a 22-year-old Anthony Edwards, faced the Denver Nuggets, the reigning NBA champions, in a seven-game series that the entire basketball world expected Denver to win. The Nuggets had Nikola Jokic, the best player on the planet. They had Jamal Murray, the most clutch playoff performer in the league. They were defending their title. Minnesota was young, energetic, and according to most predictions, not quite ready.

Nobody told Anthony Edwards. He averaged nearly 28 points per game across the series, hit shots when the games were on the line, and in Games 1 and 2 of the series put up back-to-back 40-point performances that put him in the company of Kobe Bryant as the only players aged 22 or younger to score 40 points in consecutive playoff games. The Wolves won Game 7 in Denver and knocked out the defending champions. It was the franchise's first second-round series win in exactly 20 years. The building in Minneapolis erupted. Social media erupted. The state of Minnesota erupted.

16. Crunch the Wolf: The NBA's Most Unhinged Employee

Every NBA team has a mascot. Most mascots wave to kids, shoot t-shirts into the crowd, and stand around looking enthusiastic. Crunch the Wolf, the official mascot of the Minnesota Timberwolves, has been doing all of that since 2003 and also once knocked a man clean off his seat while sledding down the arena stairs at full speed during a timeout stunt.

The victim in that 2017 incident was Karl-Anthony Towns Sr., the father of Timberwolves star Karl-Anthony Towns. Crunch was executing his signature sled run down the Target Center staircase, lost control, slammed into an empty seat in the front row, and the impact sent Towns Sr. to the floor clutching his knee. He left on crutches and later required an MRI. The team quietly retired the sled stunt. Nobody told them to stop the stunts entirely, just the sled. Crunch is still out there every game night, operating somewhere between professional entertainer and force of nature.

His origin story, as told by the team, is completely wonderful. According to Timberwolves lore, Crunch was born in the northernmost wilderness of Minnesota, taught himself basketball using a makeshift hoop made of pine cones and birch bark, and migrated south to Minneapolis when the expansion team arrived. Nobody knows where he lives inside Target Center, but legend has it there is a den somewhere deep in the building. He is summoned each game night by the howl of the fans. His pre-game meal, listed in his official NBA bio, is bacon-wrapped bacon. Crunch was inducted into the Mascot Hall of Fame in 2021 and was once named the NBA Mascot of the Year. He is one of the best in the business, even when he is accidentally sending people to hospital.

17. Prince: The Greatest Fan in Franchise History

If you were going to design the perfect superfan for the Minnesota Timberwolves, you would probably start with someone who knew the team's roster better than most coaches, watched every game from courtside with enormous sunglasses on and said almost nothing to anyone, and was also one of the most famous musicians on the planet. You would basically design Prince.

Prince Rogers Nelson was born and raised in Minneapolis and spent his entire career based in the Twin Cities, building his legendary Paisley Park recording complex just outside the city. He also happened to be completely obsessed with basketball and the Timberwolves. He played pickup games his whole life, he showed up to Timberwolves games in full regalia, and teammates from the KG era still talk about what it was like to look up and see him sitting courtside in a parka, watching only the Wolves' offensive end of the floor because he simply could not be bothered with what the other team was doing. Sam Cassell, who played in Minnesota during the 2003-04 golden season, recalled looking over at Prince during a game against the Lakers and realizing the musician was not watching Shaquille O'Neal or Kobe Bryant at all. He was only focused on the Timberwolves. As Cassell put it, Prince was cold.

In the early 1990s, Prince was reportedly part of a group that explored buying the Timberwolves to keep the franchise in Minnesota when it was nearly sold and relocated. The group also included Magic Johnson and the legendary Minneapolis production duo Jimmy Jam and Terry Lewis. The deal never happened, but the fact that Prince Rogers Nelson once tried to buy the

Timberwolves is the most Minnesota thing that has ever occurred. When Prince passed away in 2016, the Timberwolves eventually released special purple City Edition jerseys in his honor, designed in collaboration with the Prince estate and featuring fonts lifted directly from the Purple Rain album cover. They brought those jerseys back for the 2025-26 season because some things are just too good to retire.

18. The Logo That Grew Up

The first Minnesota Timberwolves logo was designed by a man named Mark Thompson from Austin, Minnesota, who submitted his drawing to a public contest and won over 2,600 entries from as far away as Alaska and Norway. Team president Bob Stein described the winning design as aggressive but not sinister. It featured a wolf mid-howl, lunging forward, and it came with a note that it was revealed to the public on an oversized $20,000 check donated to the United Way. That is one of the better debut stories in logo history.

By 1996, the team felt it needed a tougher look and introduced a redesigned logo featuring a snarling wolf looming over a field of pine trees, with black added to the color scheme. The new version was unveiled at the

Mall of America with lasers and smoke, because if you are going to change your logo in Minnesota in 1996, you absolutely need lasers and smoke. Then in 2017, the franchise did its second major overhaul, introducing a howling wolf facing forward alongside the North Star, with a color palette designed to reflect the actual landscape of Minnesota. Every color was chosen to represent something real about the state. The blue for the sky. The green for the forests. The colors that have changed tell the story of a franchise that started scrappy, got serious, and eventually decided to be proud of exactly where it came from.

19. Cold Facts About a Cold City

Minneapolis is not warm. This is not an opinion. This is a meteorological fact that Stephon Marbury reportedly had strong feelings about during his two and a half seasons there, and that multiple players over the years have politely described as a significant lifestyle adjustment. The average January temperature in Minneapolis is around 16 degrees Fahrenheit, which is minus nine in Celsius for anyone keeping score internationally. The city has more than enough days per year where the wind chill makes going outside feel like a personal insult.

What is remarkable is what the city does with this. Minneapolis consistently ranks as one of the most livable cities in America despite the cold, with world class restaurants, a thriving music and arts scene, and an infrastructure of skyways connecting downtown buildings so people can walk from their parking garage to Target Center to a restaurant without ever setting foot outside in January. There are miles of heated, connected walkways downtown. The city essentially built an indoor neighborhood so that basketball fans would not have to choose between going to a Timberwolves game and having functioning fingers. That is commitment to sport.

Remember, Minnesota has the largest wolf population in the continental United States outside of Alaska. And those 10,000 actual lakes. The team is not just named after a concept. The timberwolf is a real, active, thriving presence in the state. Every time the Wolves howl at Target Center, the wolves up north in the forests are completely unaware and doing their own thing, but the spirit is correct.

20. The Fans Who Never Left

There is a particular kind of fan that only comes from a franchise that has tested its supporters' patience to the absolute outer limits. The kind of fan who sat through the early expansion years going 22 and 60, who watched the greatest player in franchise history leave for Boston, who survived 14 consecutive years without a playoff appearance, and who still showed up, still renewed their season tickets, still howled at the appropriate moments even when the appropriate moments were rare. That is a Timberwolves fan.

The fanbase set an NBA attendance record in their very first season, cramming 49,551 people into a dome designed for football just to see a losing expansion team play its final home game. They kept the building loud during the KG years. They kept the faith during the long drought. And when Anthony Edwards arrived and started doing things that made national television analysts lose their composure, they were ready. The howl at Target Center during the 2024 playoff run against Denver was as loud as anything in the NBA that postseason. The fans had waited 20 years for that noise to matter. They had the receipts.

If you are a Wolves fan reading this book, you have earned every good moment that is coming. The winters are long. The wait has been longer. But the pack is assembled, the franchise has its star, and the howling at Target Center these days sounds like a fanbase that truly believes it. Because it does.

21. Ant-Man and the Full-Time Job of Being Anthony Edwards

Anthony Edwards became the face of the Minnesota Timberwolves at 19 years old and has been conducting himself like someone who has done this job before, which makes no sense given that he had not. By his fourth season he was an All-NBA player, an All-Star, the number one option on a team with a legitimate championship core, and the most entertaining postgame interview in the entire league. He averaged 25.9 points per game in 2023-24 and was seventh in MVP voting. He was 22 years old.

The numbers are one thing. The personality is another. Edwards is the rare superstar who makes the people around him better while also being completely, sincerely hilarious in a way that does not feel like a media training exercise. When asked once how long it would take him to become the best player in the NBA, he thought about it for approximately half a second and said two or three years. This is not arrogance in the way that reads poorly. This is the kind of supreme confidence that you only find in players who back it up on the court every single night, and Edwards does. He has passed Karl-Anthony Towns for the most 40-point games in franchise history. He has surpassed Kevin Garnett for the most 30-point playoff games in Wolves history. He is 24 years old and he is just getting started.

The other thing about Ant is that he loves Minnesota. Actually loves it. He stays in the offseason. He invests in the community. He is the franchise in a way that goes beyond the stats, and the fans understand that. Kevin Garnett was the soul of the Timberwolves for 12 years. Anthony Edwards is auditioning to be the soul of the Timberwolves for the next 15.

22. The Trade That Shocked Everyone, Including the Players

In July 2022, the Minnesota Timberwolves called Utah Jazz center Rudy Gobert and told him he was being traded to Minnesota. Gobert, a three-time Defensive Player of the Year who had spent nine seasons in Utah, was reportedly surprised. His new teammates were reportedly surprised. Rival executives around the league were surprised. The price tag was staggering: five players and five first-round draft picks, which is the kind of trade cost that makes sensible basketball people sit down and breathe slowly.

The new ownership group of Alex Rodriguez and Marc Lore, who agreed to buy the Timberwolves for 1.5 billion dollars in 2021 over homemade burgers at the previous owner's Florida home, approved the Gobert trade in roughly five minutes after their basketball operations president Tim Connelly brought it to them. Five minutes. Most people take longer than that to order at a restaurant. The national media reaction was swift and brutal. Multiple analysts called it an overpay. One noted ESPN writer wrote a column arguing it was going to be a disaster. The first season with Gobert was rocky enough that it looked like they might be right.

Then something shifted. The team built an elite defense around Gobert's rim protection. Anthony Edwards elevated. The roster clicked. Minnesota made the Western Conference Finals in 2024 for the first time since 2004. They made it again in 2025. The Gobert trade went from punchline to foundation piece. The analyst who wrote the disaster column has not taken it back publicly, but some things speak for themselves.

23. A New Pack Forms

When Karl-Anthony Towns was traded to the New York Knicks in the autumn of 2024, the reaction in Minnesota was somewhere between stunned silence and full-scale alarm. KAT had been the anchor of the franchise for nine seasons. He was popular, dominant, and had only just started playing the best basketball of his career alongside Edwards. Then, for salary cap reasons connected to the new luxury tax rules and a roster that had become one of the most expensive in the league, he was gone. In return, the Wolves received Julius Randle and Donte DiVincenzo from New York.

It was not the trade anyone had planned. Randle, a powerful scoring forward, brought a different kind of skill set and a different kind of energy to the locker room. DiVincenzo brought shooting and defensive versatility. Neither of them was Karl-Anthony Towns. But basketball rosters are not built on sentiment. They are built on what works. The Wolves had a core around Edwards and Gobert that had already proven it could reach conference finals. The question for the post-KAT era was not whether they were good enough to compete. They already knew they were. The question was whether they were good enough to take that final step.

Edwards handled the transition the way he handles everything, by walking into practice, being himself, and making it clear that the standards in Minnesota were not going down. He had been the heir apparent for years. Now he was simply the king.

24. The Ownership Bet and the Billion Dollar Handshake

In 2021, a retired baseball superstar and a technology entrepreneur sat down to eat homemade burgers in a Florida home and agreed to buy the Minnesota Timberwolves for 1.5 billion dollars. The previous owner, Glen Taylor, wrote his asking price on a piece of paper, slid it across the table, and that was essentially how the deal started. Alex Rodriguez, who won a World Series title in 2009 and 14 All-Star selections as a player, brought the star power. Marc Lore, who built and sold multiple companies including Jet.com to Walmart for 3.3 billion dollars, brought the business firepower. Together they inherited a franchise in the middle of a genuine resurgence and set about making sure it stayed that way.

The transition was not entirely smooth. There were ownership disputes, arbitration proceedings, and more legal drama than most NBA franchise sales generate. But by 2025 the deal was finalized, the new owners were in place, and the Timberwolves had new money, new ambition, and a fanbase that was excited about where things were heading. Rodriguez had watched championship parades up close during his playing career. He knew what one looked like. Minneapolis has never had one. The city is ready.

25. The Hunt for the First Championship

The Minnesota Timberwolves have never been to the NBA Finals. This is a fact that sits in the back of every fan's mind like a song stuck on repeat. They have been close. They made the Western Conference Finals in 2004 and lost to a Lakers team that had Shaquille O'Neal and Kobe Bryant in their prime. They went back to the conference finals in 2024 and 2025 before falling to the Dallas Mavericks and then the Oklahoma City Thunder respectively. Each time the door opened, something pushed it shut.

But here is what is different now compared to any other point in franchise history. They have a 24-year-old superstar who has quickly turned the Wolves into a consistent playoff team, plays better in big moments than he does in small ones, and explicitly said he is not yet close to his prime. They have an ownership group with deep pockets and championship hunger. They have a coaching staff that knows how to build a defensive identity that travels in the playoffs. And they have a fanbase that has endured more heartbreak than any team in the league and is still showing up every single night, howling.

Every championship has to come eventually. No franchise suffers forever. The Minneapolis Lakers won five titles between 1949 and 1954. The city knows what championship basketball feels like even if it was before most of its residents were born. The Timberwolves have never won it. But the pack is assembled. The star is young. The hunger is real.

Minnesota is waiting. And Anthony Edwards does not like to keep people waiting.

Bonus Trivia Quiz!

You think you are a true Timberwolves fan? Try this bonus quiz!

1. What were the two finalist names in the public contest to name Minnesota's new NBA team?

A) Timberwolves and Blizzards
B) Timberwolves and Polars
C) Timberwolves and Northstars
D) Timberwolves and Lumberjacks

2. How much did Harvey Ratner and Marv Wolfenson pay for the expansion franchise in 1987?

A) $20 million
B) $50 million
C) $32.5 million
D) $45 million

3. What record did the Timberwolves set during their very first home season at the Metrodome?

A) Most wins by an expansion team
B) Largest attendance at a single NBA game
C) First expansion team to make the playoffs
D) Most points scored in a single season

4. Kevin Garnett was the first player drafted directly from high school in how many years when Minnesota picked him in 1995?

A) 10 years

B) 15 years

C) 20 years

D) 25 years

5. What was Kevin Garnett's nickname during his time with the Timberwolves?

A) The Franchise

B) The Big Ticket

C) The Minnesota Kid

D) The Wolf King

6. Stephon Marbury was traded to Minnesota on draft night in 1996 in exchange for which player?

A) Latrell Sprewell

B) Sam Cassell

C) Ray Allen

D) Terrell Brandon

7. What was Kevin Love's most famous single-game performance as a Timberwolf?

A) 51 points and 14 rebounds against Oklahoma City
B) 31 points and 31 rebounds against the New York Knicks
C) 40 points and 20 rebounds against the LA Lakers
D) 45 points and 18 rebounds against the Chicago Bulls

8. In the 2003-04 MVP season, how many points, rebounds and assists per game did Kevin Garnett average?

A) 22.1 points, 11.2 rebounds, 4.1 assists
B) 26.0 points, 12.5 rebounds, 4.8 assists
C) 24.2 points, 13.9 rebounds, 5.0 assists
D) 23.7 points, 14.1 rebounds, 3.9 assists

9. Which veteran players did the Timberwolves bring in to support Kevin Garnett during the 2003-04 season?

A) Gary Payton and Karl Malone
B) Sam Cassell and Latrell Sprewell
C) Jason Kidd and Vince Carter
D) Steve Nash and Rasheed Wallace

10. Karl-Anthony Towns scored 60 points in a 2022 game against which team?

A) Los Angeles Lakers

B) New York Knicks

C) San Antonio Spurs

D) Golden State Warriors

11. What famous musician was one of the most well-known courtside fans in Timberwolves history?

A) Bob Dylan

B) Usher

C) Prince

D) Bruce Springsteen

12. What happened when Timberwolves mascot Crunch was performing his sled stunt in 2017?

A) He slid into the opposing team's bench

B) He accidentally injured Karl-Anthony Towns Sr.

C) He crashed into a referee

D) He knocked over the shot clock

13. How many first-round draft picks did Minnesota send to Utah as part of the Rudy Gobert trade in 2022?

A) Three

B) Four

C) Five

D) Six

14. After eliminating the Denver Nuggets in the 2024 playoffs, what did Anthony Edwards tell Charles Barkley on national television?

A) Minnesota is the greatest city in America

B) Tell Nikola Jokic we said hi

C) ring ya ass

D) We are just getting started

15. Who purchased the Minnesota Timberwolves from longtime owner Glen Taylor, completing the sale in 2025 for 1.5 billion dollars?

A) Jeff Bezos and Jay-Z

B) Alex Rodriguez and Marc Lore

C) LeBron James and Maverick Carter

D) Michael Bloomberg and Dan Gilbert

Super Fan Secret Challenge

Only a true Timberwolves fan will know this.

(No Answer Provided)

Only the most dedicated Wolves fans will know this one. Kevin Garnett won the NBA Player of the Month award four times in a single season during his 2003-04 MVP campaign. But here is the real question. In the 2002-03 season, Garnett became only the third player in NBA history to lead his team in all five major statistical categories in the same season: points, rebounds, assists, steals, and blocks. Two players had done it before him. Name both of them.

A) Bill Russell and Wilt Chamberlain
B) Dave Cowens and Scottie Pippen
C) Oscar Robertson and Larry Bird
D) Magic Johnson and Charles Barkley

Answer Key

1. B) Timberwolves and Polars

2. C) $32.5 million

3. B) Largest attendance at a single NBA game

4. C) 20 years

5. B) The Big Ticket

6. C) Ray Allen

7. B) 31 points and 31 rebounds against the New York Knicks

8. C) 24.2 points, 13.9 rebounds, 5.0 assists

9. B) Sam Cassell and Latrell Sprewell

10. C) San Antonio Spurs

11. C) Prince

12. B) He accidentally injured Karl-Anthony Towns Sr.

13. C) Five

14. C) ring ya ass

15. B) Alex Rodriguez and Marc Lore

NBA PLAYOFF BRACKET

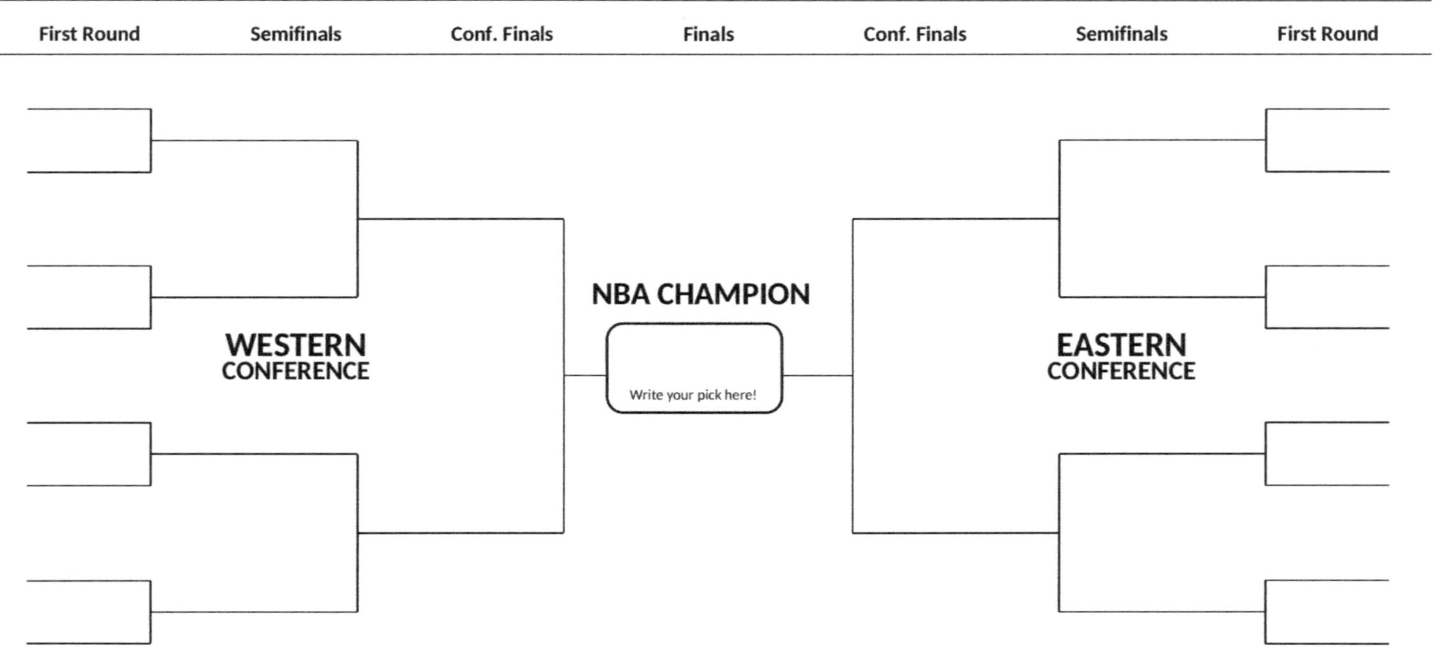

* Fill in your picks and try not to argue with your friends about it!

Part of the Fun Fan Facts: The Unofficial Sports Guide Series

Be the Boss of the Playoffs

You've broken down the matchups. You know which superstar takes over in the fourth quarter. You've seen the bench units that quietly decide series. You've watched the adjustments coaches make when their backs are against the wall.

Now it's time to stop watching and start deciding.

On this page, you are not just a fan. You are the Head Coach drawing up the last play with three seconds left on the clock. You are the GM who built this roster. You are the analyst who saw it all coming.

This is not just filling out a bracket.

This is building your championship run.

Sixteen teams enter the NBA Playoffs. The path is brutal. Best of seven. No shortcuts. No hiding. Every round gets louder, harder, and more personal.

This bracket is your Playoff Control Room.

The Game Plan

1. Survive Round One: Start with the opening round. Which matchup is going seven games? Who has the closer? Who folds under pressure? Make the calls.

2. Feel the Momentum: As you move into the Conference Semifinals and Conference Finals, things change. Role players become heroes. Stars feel the weight. Trust your reads.

3. Own the Finals: Trace your picks all the way to the NBA Finals. When the confetti falls and the trophy is raised, you'll find out who earned it.

House Rules: Circle your boldest upset. That is your official "I knew it" moment.

Choose Your Weapon: Pencil if you want flexibility. Pen if you trust your instincts. Sharpie if you believe in chaos.

Because once the playoffs tip off, there is no rewinding Game 7.

Make your picks. Trust your basketball brain. And let the playoff drama begin.

Fun Facts Wrap-Up

You made it through! You're officially a true superfan! Now it's time to put your knowledge to the test. Share these facts with friends and see who really knows their team best.

Love the series?

Your reviews help other fans discover Fun Fan Facts. If you enjoyed this book, we'd really appreciate you sharing your thoughts and leaving a review.

Want more Fun Fan Facts?

Scan the QR code below to visit our site and explore bonus trivia, challenges, and special extras - including new teams, future series, and collectible fun as they're released.

Collect All the Fun Fan Facts Series!

Check off every book you read. See the full set on Amazon. Search "Fun Fan Facts Jake Liam."

World Cup 2026 Edition

☐ Algeria	☐ France	☐ Paraguay
☐ Argentina	☐ Germany	☐ Portugal
☐ Australia	☐ Ghana	☐ Qatar
☐ Austria	☐ Haiti	☐ Saudi Arabia
☐ Belgium	☐ Iran	☐ Scotland
☐ Brazil	☐ Ivory Coast	☐ Senegal
☐ Canada	☐ Japan	☐ South Africa
☐ Cape Verde	☐ Jordan	☐ South Korea
☐ Colombia	☐ Mexico	☐ Spain
☐ Croatia	☐ Morocco	☐ Switzerland
☐ Curaçao	☐ Netherlands	☐ Tunisia
☐ Ecuador	☐ New Zealand	☐ United States
☐ Egypt	☐ Norway	☐ Uruguay
☐ England	☐ Panama	☐ Uzbekistan

World Cup 2026 Group Edition

☐ Group A	☐ Group E	☐ Group I
☐ Group B	☐ Group F	☐ Group J
☐ Group C	☐ Group G	☐ Group K
☐ Group D	☐ Group H	☐ Group L

English Football Edition

☐ Arsenal F.C.	☐ Manchester City
☐ Aston Villa F.C.	☐ Manchester United
☐ Chelsea F.C.	☐ Newcastle United F.C.
☐ Everton F.C.	☐ Tottenham Hotspur
☐ Fulham F.C.	☐ West Ham United
☐ Liverpool F.C.	☐ Wrexham A.F.C.

NBA Edition

☐ Atlanta Hawks	☐ Miami Heat
☐ Boston Celtics	☐ Milwaukee Bucks
☐ Brooklyn Nets	☐ Minnesota Timberwolves
☐ Charlotte Hornets	☐ New Orleans Pelicans
☐ Chicago Bulls	☐ New York Knicks
☐ Cleveland Cavaliers	☐ Oklahoma City Thunder
☐ Dallas Mavericks	☐ Orlando Magic
☐ Denver Nuggets	☐ Philadelphia 76ers
☐ Detroit Pistons	☐ Phoenix Suns
☐ Golden State Warriors	☐ Portland Trail Blazers
☐ Houston Rockets	☐ Sacramento Kings
☐ Indiana Pacers	☐ San Antonio Spurs
☐ LA Clippers	☐ Toronto Raptors
☐ Los Angeles Lakers	☐ Utah Jazz
☐ Memphis Grizzlies	☐ Washington Wizards

About the Author

Jake is a 13-year-old sports fan who loves football, American football, and basketball. He plays soccer as a goalie and dreams of one day playing for West Ham United and helping teach kids to love the game. His passion for sports runs in the family - his dad was a professional baseball player, and his stepdad sparked his love for West Ham. Through the Fun Fan Facts series, he shares the fun and excitement of sports with fans everywhere.

www.ingramcontent.com/pod-product-compliance
Lightning Source LLC
Chambersburg PA
CBHW050040040726
47599CB00015B/1766